Unedited

Volume III

Dr. Jai

BookLeaf Publishing

Presentation by *BookLeaf Publishing*

Web: www.bookleafpub.com

E-mail: info@bookleafpub.com

ISBN: 9789357214896

First edition 2022

I dedicate this work of art to my grandparents, parents, and the next generations to come. Be unstoppable and know that you are the creator of your life. Create deliberately and beautifully.

ACKNOWLEDGEMENT

I must first acknowledge God - the Universe, the Divine, Oneness. Love is God and God is love. I then must acknowledge my "SELF." I am grateful for all of the SELF love, SELF awareness, SELF growth and grace that I have gained throughout my life journey. Lastly, I must always honor my ancestors and elders who holds light on the path that I walk daily.

PREFACE

These poems are another round of unscripted thoughts, feelings and emotions that are illuminated from within, without a need to be written grammatically correct. This is the final chapter of the Unedited series with the theme of transparency, allowing light to pass through the darkness of life.

SEE-quences

A beginning, a middle, and an end
It is a knowing that everything has this sequence
We emerge in the world as infants, survive/thrive and then die
Only to find out our existence never ends

I started reading esoteric books and it revealed new knowledge
Somethings my own reality can't even acknowledge
Like how by design our minds are born into a cottage
Or a specific condition that introduces to us the perception of physical reality
That includes: our sexuality, mentality, and the perspective of duality
But in our ever-changing consciousness, we experience immortality

It is by design we allow perception to create our reality
But when we sleep, we experience a universality

Where we travel to the many realms of existence
That would normally be blocked by our conscious mind

As its job is to keep us confined, blind, and inclined to just materialization
But we must experience something like a bacterial invasion
Where we allow the subconscious to invade all systems of our being
It is when we awaken the closed eye that we are foreseeing
And we set ourselves free

So that in the end, we can have a jubilee
And then sail across the sky in the sea
Only to be reminded that the beginning, middle, and end is a continuous three

SEE-quences…

Rhythm & Harm0ny

Information
Education
Generation
Change a nation

Participation
Consideration
Transformation
Conversation

All should handle our situation
But we forgot our imagination
To busy worrying about our reputation
We miss the nudge of inspiration
And instead experience modification
Replacing inspiration for motivation
And this fucks up our liberation
Now we are in church looking for revelation
Because we replaced the joy of the journey with the destination

So now we are back to meditation
As we work to lift our vibration
From all of the worldly deprivation
And the self-inflicted harm (i.e. intoxication)

Not to mention the race war annihilation

Releasing all of this, looking up at the constellation
Finding something to focus our concentration
Opening our hearts feeling the sensation
As we move to the state of love, elevation

Learning there never was any expectation
God is within us looking with admiration
So we can be all that we are through illumination
Only to realize we were the foolish humans creating complications…

Contribution 2 Society

What is my contribution to society?
This connects to my 10th house ruler Saturn
How about I take a second to analyze my pattern?
I'm impeccable with my words
Writing fire from this pen forming predicate and verbs
So sharp and pristine the words that I write
Oftentimes, I repeat them and see them forming my life

The million-dollar question is as follows:
What is my contribution to society?
I use my words to heal the addictions of others, sobriety
And to send spiritual energy helping people calm their anxiety
And to live a life of expanded consciousness and create beautiful realities, variety

I like to think of my words as therapy to others, psychiatry
And this love and magic I write uplift the world and high societies

It will be impossible to quiet me with the
vibration of Dr. Jai

So I write it in my diary, before I say
Because being authentic and courageous is what
I am, I have no choice
With my contributions to society, my fellow
men and women will rejoice

And remember, the vibration of words come
straight from my voice…

Dating Technology

I am writing the 21st century chronicles
Unfortunately, this information is not available in the current periodicals
Of how the new world of errors came into existence
Now every relationship is basically long distance

No such thing as physical relationships, they are nonexistent
I'm talking about our new relationships with technology
Those are our new boyfriends and girlfriends

Haven't you heard the news?
We are now dating technology
We send nudes to bae every second of the day
We write him or her a love letter in 140 characters

Our new relationships are basically open
Where we have thousands of lovers and some undercover
Who are committed to other technological lovers

But that don't stop her from getting under the covers
She'll Facetime you for passionate, wild, steamy sext
And move right on to the next

We don't go out on casual dates anymore
We just take ourselves to a place with an epic background
Pull our cameras out and do a wrap-around

it's more appealing…

Now in the 21st century, the main goal is to have no feelings
And that helps us avoid any and all type of healing
Because we don't want any trace of our authentic self, revealing
As we date technology

When have humans turned away from astrology?
Well, at least we don't have to worry about an apology
Because our new boyfriends and girlfriends have no biology…

Self Questioning

When you start to ask yourself "WHY?"
There is no place you can run and hide
You soon realize that it brings clarity and inner peace
It somehow starts to gently tame that inner beast
The one that has been blaming others not taking responsibility
You know, the one that don't believe in accountability

The one who sees themself as a victim of life which brings about self-agony
When all they had to do was utilize the law of analogy
Which causes one to self-analyze and find the patterns of their demise
So that they can be like the phoenix and rise
Which is no surprise

When you ask the question "WHY" you become whole again
And can see your own formula
Never being afraid to repeat steps one through ten

The formula comes from within
And is available to all men…

Metaphysical Assertions

Metaphysics
Metaphysical
Why is everything so political?

Don't you know everything isn't physical
But your mind is so analytical
So you become critical

You've killed your connection to the spiritual
By cutting the cord, umbilical
Rooted in 3D reality, empirical
Forgetting the power of words, lyrical

Now you're experiencing depression, clinal
Hmm, humans are so typical
You let your low energy win, egotistical
And forgot how to be mystical

You are no longer a child, whimsical
You ask: What happens when you don't tap into the nonphysical?

I answered: You are unable to become indivisible…

Pen Pal = God

God is my pen pal
So I can never fail
He knows my inner thoughts
All of the words coming from my heart
He writes me back in verses
His words are authentic, he never rehearses

His writing is so clear it forms mental pictures
He frees me from the confines of my mind
And when he writes me, we are on primordial time
It's like I transform into Alice and I'm in wonderland

He constantly writes me a new game plan
One that is filled with the best routes
So I never have to worry about the traps of humanly conditions and doubts

God is my pen pal
And with that I have superior intel
I will always prevail
He gives me life in every detail
Through the writing of his verses

I enjoy the way me and God constantly converses…

The Dark-ness

I have this new ritual of sitting in the dark
With the attempts of activating my zone of genius to light a spark
It helps me to slow down the millions of thoughts that run through my mind
For the solid, magical ones that I am trying to find

This ritual allows me to be one with time
So that I can define the inner workings of my mind's design
I sit in the dark because it brings me quietness
I'm tired of the conflict between my mind and heart with its one sidedness
I'm just trying to slaughter my animalistic nature like a lioness
As I activate my dot of consciousness to meet God like a diocese

I am grateful for the understanding and the ability to sit in the dark
Isn't that how Noah built his arc?
As I travel through the journey of my soul to find my spark

And to swim across the ocean of my fears like a
shark
And to purposefully use my magic to elevate
my consciousness like John Henrik Clarke…

TrUth

The truth is behind the facts
You have to get those lies in check
Facts are easy to quote and pass of as a lie
But look me directly in my eyes

And tell the truth that cannot be unheard
My ears are paying attention to all of your words
And my heart intercepted the energy that was transferred

So please before you formulate a sentence
Make sure you are speaking the truth
Stop and think long and hard like you did in your youth
If that fails think about the bible story of Ruth

Because there is truth behind the facts
And I can see behind all of your acts

Tell me the truth…

H0me

Home, oh how I've long
To take that journey to you
Where my heart can smile
And I reveal what I would normally hide

A Black woman living in a White world
Trying to hold her chest out and stride
Like a lioness roaming the jungle with pride
Realizing that in this world she can't hide

She must take home with her
Because when home is realized and valued
She is unstoppable and vulnerable
Which makes her the most powerful
person on the planet

No, I'm not talking about Janet
But the Jack sun that rise everyday
Helping us to make a way
In this beautiful world

That we fold up with music
artificial beauty and good sex
Without going deeper within

We are forever longing for home

Only to realize that it was never gone…

The Journey To...

The journey to
Is filled with confidence

The journey to
Is filled with pain

The journey to
Is sometimes done in vain

The journey to
Is sometimes misleading

The journey to
Is also fleeting

The journey to
Keeps you asking questions

The journey to
Leaves you second guessing

The journey to
Sometimes disappoints you

The journey to

Is filled with so much unknown

The journey to
Leave you moving with no home

The journey to
Loves you so much

The journey to
Taught you how to trust

The journey to
Helps you meet new souls

The journey to
Keeps giving you new goals

The journey to
Makes you miss out on family events

The journey to
Protects you from the illusions

The journey to
Causes new illusions to emerge

The journey to
Loves to lead from the mind

The journey to
Is on a path to find

Your heart. Your purpose. Your mission. Your voice…

Pathologies

The presence of maladaptive behaviors
Are what we call family pathologies
They are classified as different scenarios within the bloodline
But you see them constantly sometimes in the vein from them cutlines
Not far fetch that she's standing on the corner in the bus line
As she was born into such reality of standing in a tough line

Having to pick a side as jealously and fighting between siblings occur
But coming from a healthy, loving, abundant family is what she prefers
Like a lot of Black families, she has relatives locked up for murder
She broke the generational curse and obtained her first degree

Mental illness runs within the circle of elders such as schizophrenia
Causing more confusion and relatives to interpret reality abnormally

But fuck, can she escape all the family pathologies formally?
To live a life of normalcy

She found out that it's possible by not giving in to conformity
On her way to Normandy to give a normal speech
She realized that all old programming and patterns were breached
Now she is able to travel the world and teach

Goodbye family pathologies
Hello newly develop knowledge and qualities
We are no longer giving out apologies

Because we healed those generational traumas and pathologies…

Life & The Jungle

Born and raised in the jungle with other lions
The main objective was survival
As poverty in consciousness is the vicious cycle
That keeps the patterns of deprivation current
Who would've thought we would make it out of the jungle?
The pride that studied the environment and decided differently
Who created a masterful plan with God deliberately

The other lions are no longer content with the jungle
They want to kill and attack the thrivers who were once survivors
Not knowing that you are in the front seat as the driver
You don't have to be in the jungle with other lions and tigers
Constantly on guard of being attacked or killed by its prey

You can decide today

To leave the jungle and find a new environment conducive to your growth
Instead of living in the jungle a life that you loath
Honestly, all we did was take an oath

To want to live a different life of ease, abundance, and prosperity
But you must focus your attention and find the clarity
That comes through solidarity and sincerity

So in the end, instead of being a lion you can be a bird
Flying freely in the air, without saying a word
The path is always clear and the lines are never blurred

You can go from being a lion to a bird…

Vodka, Cigarettes & Soda

So I was looking at someone's birthday picture
And I couldn't help but notice the background

I saw a bottle of vodka, a soda, and a cigarette
All of which are substances to make us forget
Causing our nervous system cells to get upset
Let alone these items possess a bigger threat

To our vibrational frequency and subtle bodies
As we lose the thought of being carbon copies
of God's creative design of the galaxy
Because we were taught to believe the fallacy
That we are inferior with our black exterior

So we put alcohol and other toxic substances in our sacred temples
Just to give you a self-destructive vivid example
Remember it all starts with a sample
Just one drink, one hit, and one taste
Causing all our regenerative cells to go to waste

So please remember next time you want a taste
That you are a version of God here on Earth not in space…

See Me?

When you look at me what do you see?
Do you see the love in my heart?
Do you see the values I hold?
Do you see the stars in my eyes?
Do you see energy in my vocal cords?
How about the flow of my thoughts?

Do you see the motion picture of my childhood?
How about my transformation to womanhood?
Do you see the purpose I hold?
How about a mind that is gold?

NO…

What you see is the color of my skin
You see the size of my body
Those are your precursors to respect me or not
Or to decide if I'm worth your standard

You then ask me about my career and degrees
But none of those are guarantees of my value
And if you must know, I am someone you can't
devalue

I know, I know, that probably shocked you

The lesson here is to never knock her
There is more than what meets the eyes

It is all of my internal attributes that will leave you surprised…

DamN Mind

Damn Mind,

Why won't you let me be happy
and follow my heart without any interference?
There is a conflict between you and my heart
I want to follow my heart but you always bring up the past
That depicts my lack of experience with love and relationships
It's like you purposely try to sabotage every good connection

Why won't you let me be happy?
I can no longer survive with you in complete isolation
I am human and by design, I need to make other connections
I can no longer follow any of your directions
But I will keep my last relationship alive just for reflections

Because I want to love wholly without any objections
And to do that, I must terminate our isolated toxic connection

This time, I allow my heart to rule because I
need love and affection

And we are all human, so I must look past all of
my imperfections

So long mind, I choose to be happy
You can save all those negative thoughts no
need to get snappy

Because my heart is all about love so it will
never get scrappy…

Beneath The Layer(s)

What exist beneath the layers?
It's like being in the forest and opening the bushes to a new world
It reminds me of the scene of Alice in wonderland
Where she crossed into another dimension

Will I finally be able to see my being's consciousness extension?
You know the freeing of the mind's comprehension and tension
Of course, I'm now experiencing all of this energetic suspension
I see auras, and electromagnetic waves, everything is floating against gravity I can even feel my heart beating and expanding outside of my chest cavity
It's like I am beyond the forces of nature and supergravity
Can this always be my reality?

When you operate from the inner ego there are no limitations of 3D reality
It's like all old programming and thoughts go out the window neutrality

And there is an enhanced vitality, the thoughts of morality are obsolete

My friend, you have experienced what it feels like to be complete
After this astral journey, nothing will feel concrete
We are forever traveling within dimensions, isn't that a sweet treat?

And the goal is to keep this astral journey experience on repeat...

D0mestication Proce$$

What is your process of domestication?
It is a learned behavior just as we learn about multiplication
It is behaviors, ideas, and childhood programming that compounds
And those negative thoughts that you act out when no one is around

Because you believe everything you think
And you believe that those thoughts are the real you without a blink
So, what is your process of domestication?

That fear that impedes you from achieving your greatness
Not taking action and holding back words, afraid to speak with straightness
So instead, you walk around miserable thinking all is doomed
Not realizing that once you free yourself from domestication you will blossom and bloom

And the beauty of your dreams and hopes will resume

Because you freed yourself from the outdated ideas, patterns, and behaviors that you accepted during the domestication process

Realizing that it's time to transcend to heaven from hell
It was just a matter of perspective and freeing yourself from the cell
Look at you thriving, life is beautiful once you freed yourself from mental jail

As they say in the bible, only the strong will prevail…

Children @ The Park

The children are playing at the park
What surrounds me are smiles and worry-free faces
I see kids of all classes, ages and races
They are still pure in essence and have not decided to hate others
I guess love was instilled early on in the home by their mothers

I ponder on the thought of when does differences matter
Because trauma causes shooters to go in schools and blood splatters
I'm hoping that the innocence will remain
And none these children are bullied or their names said in vain
Or they experience pain that causes rage to rise in their veins

The children are playing at the park
All I see are smiles and hear words of positive remark
I wish to see this joy remain for a lifetime in their little hearts

And I hope this innocence will one day light a spark

We could all benefit from children playing at the park...

AuthentiCITY

We grow up learning from those around us
Even if they begin to down us

We embody everything that they do
Until they leave us and now you are feeling blue
And you are left with only you

It is in those moments
You begin to shed
Liked a lion
You roam the streets looking for bread

The bread of knowledge
That helps you grow
So you can evolve from being poor

Poor in spirit and filled with old programming
You wake up to your authenticity

And when you do
You can never go back
To the old you
Because that programming
No longer controls you

You have emerged
As your unique self
So all of that other stuff
Can go back on the shelf

It is no longer relevant
To how you navigate in the world
So keep it moving
And let your new authentic self explore
Because now you are going to crave more

More life
More love
More meaningful connections
And everything that is not of love
  will dissipate
So please just be patient and wait

You have to adjust to your new self

But in the meantime
Go give someone some help
And praise God for authenticity
Because now you have a new synergy…

With-OUT, With-IN

Without within
You cannot win

It creates problems
And causes you to sin

Without within
There is no guide
All that does
Is forces you to hide

Without within
You don't know how to love
So you walk around
And barely give hugs

Without within
You shun human connections
It also causes you
To not recognize your blessings

Without within
You don't recognize your emotions
So you check out
And go through the motions

Without within
You can't fully comprehend
So you don't understand
The importance of zin

Without within
You rush through everything
And you find it hard
To make real friends

Without within
You cannot survive
So you walk around numb
And try to hide

But eventually

Without within catches up to you
And you realize
That the key to life is to go within
Because just living without
Is filled with so much sin

You have to calm the mind and zin
In order to successfully go within

So you can win

In your life…

www.ingramcontent.com/pod-product-compliance
Lightning Source LLC
Chambersburg PA
CBHW051741130826
49812CB00033B/953
* 9 7 8 9 3 5 7 2 1 4 8 9 6 *